W9-ASL-388

DATE DUE

How Things Are Made

Sap to Syrup

By Inez Snyder

Welcome Books™

Children's Press®
A Division of Scholastic Inc.
New York / Toronto / London / Auckland / Sydney
Mexico City / New Delhi / Hong Kong
Danbury, Connecticut

Photo Credits: Cover © Foodcollection/Stockfood America; p. 5 © Kathleen Brown/Corbis; p. 11 © Robert Maass/Corbis; pp. 13, 19 © Richard Hamilton Smith/Corbis; p. 17 © Randy M. Ury/Corbis; p. 21 © Dex Images, Inc./Corbis; pp. 7, 9, 15 © AP/Wide World Photos

Contributing Editor: Shira Laskin
Book Design: Mikhail Bortnik and Jennifer Crilly

Library of Congress Cataloging-in-Publication Data

Snyder, Inez.
   Sap to syrup / by Inez Snyder.
   p. cm. — (How things are made)
   Includes index.
   ISBN 0-516-25194-5 (lib. bdg.) — ISBN 0-516-25530-4 (pbk.)
   1. Cookery (Syrups) 2. Syrups. I. Title.

TX819.S96S68 2005
641.6'36—dc22

                                            2005003820

Contents

Syrup is made from the **sap** inside maple trees.

Sap is a **liquid** made of water and sugar.

5

First, the sap must be gathered.

A hole is drilled into the side of the tree.

A **spout** is placed in the hole.

The sap drips out of the spout.

9

A **bucket** is hung on the tree.

The sap drips into the bucket.

When enough sap has been gathered, it is taken to the **sugarhouse**.

There, the sap will be turned into syrup.

13

Inside the sugarhouse, the sap is cooked.

It must **boil**.

After the sap has boiled for a long time, it becomes thicker and darker.

Now it is syrup.

The syrup is put into bottles.

Pure
MAPLE
SYRUP
32 FL. OZ. (1 QT.)

Pure
MAPLE
SYRUP
32 FL. OZ. (1 QT.)

19

Many people like maple syrup.

It tastes great on pancakes!

21

New Words

boil (**boil**) when a liquid gets very hot and has bubbles on the surface

bucket (**buhk**-it) a round container that is open at the top

liquid (**lik**-wuhd) something wet that you can pour

sap (**sap**) the liquid, made of water and sugar, that flows through a plant, carrying water and food from one part of the plant to another

spout (**spout**) a tube placed in the side of a maple tree through which sap flows

sugarhouse (**shug**-uhr-hous) the building in which sap is boiled until it becomes syrup

syrup (**sir**-uhp) a sweet, thick liquid made from the sap of maple trees that is poured over pancakes and other foods

To Find Out More

Books

From Maple Tree to Syrup
by Melanie S. Mitchell
Lerner Publishing Group

From Tree to Table
by Susan Ring
Capstone Press, Incorporated

Web Site
Michigan Maple Syrup Association: Online Activities for Kids
http://www.mi-maplesyrup.com/Activities/activities_kids.htm
Visit this Web site for information about making maple syrup
and fun maple syrup activities.

Index

About the Author
Inez Snyder writes books to help children learn how to read.

Content Consultant
Peter Reed, Brewster Central School District, Brewster, NY

Reading Consultants
Kris Flynn, Coordinator, Small School District Literacy, The San Diego County Office of Education

Shelly Forys, Certified Reading Recovery Specialist, W.J. Zahnow Elementary School, Waterloo, IL

Paulette Mansell, Certified Reading Recovery Specialist, and Early Literacy Consultant, TX